NURTURING THE NEXT GENERATION

A GUIDE TO CHILD DEVELOPMENT AND PARENTING

SHRUTHI B S

Made with ♥ on the Notion Press Platform
www.notionpress.com

My daughter Sadhvi, who inspired me always and has taught me the true meaning of unconditional love and nurturing. Your unwavering faith and support have made me the parent I am today.

I am dedicating this book to my beloved husband Rajini Shetty. Who is stupident support for my life ever. His inspiration and caring as well as his unconditional support helped me to bring out this book

To all the parents who strive every day to do their best for their children, this book is for you. May it provide you with the guidance, support, and inspiration to navigate the wonderful, yet challenging journey of parenting.

I would also dedicate this book Smt,Ramya Suresh Shaiva and Sri Suresh Shaiva as my friend and mentor being this journey I will take their names too dedicate this book.

And to the next generation, may you grow up to be confident, resilient, and compassionate individuals, guided by the love and wisdom of your parents.

Contents

Contents

Contents

FOREWORD

Dear readers,

It is with great pleasure that I introduce this comprehensive guide to child development and parenting. This book is a testament to the dedication and love that parents have for their children, and the authors have done an excellent job of capturing the essence of what it means to be a parent.

As you delve into the pages of this book, you will find a wealth of knowledge and practical advice on how to raise healthy, happy, and well-rounded children. Whether you are a new parent, an experienced parent, or simply looking for guidance on your parenting journey, this book will provide you with valuable insights and tools to support your child's growth and development.

From physical development to emotional intelligence, from building strong relationships to supporting your child's interests, this book covers all the key areas of child development and parenting. The authors have done a fantastic job of presenting complex information in an easy-to-understand format, making it accessible to all parents, regardless of their level of education or experience.

I am honored to be a part of this book and I wholeheartedly recommend it to all parents. Whether you are seeking to deepen your understanding of child development or simply looking for new ideas and strategies to support your child, this book will not disappoint.

With gratitude and appreciation,
Suresh Shaiva
Mind Therapist

Preface

Writing a book is never a solitary journey, and this one was no exception. I would like to take a moment to acknowledge and express my gratitude to all those who have helped me bring this book to life.

Firstly, I would like to thank my family, who have supported me throughout this journey and encouraged me to pursue my passion for writing and sharing my knowledge on parenting. Their unwavering support and encouragement have been instrumental in keeping me motivated and inspired.

I am also grateful to my friends who have listened to me, offered their opinions, and helped me shape my ideas into a coherent book. Your input has been invaluable and I am deeply thankful for your support and guidance.

I would also like to acknowledge the countless experts and researchers in the field of child development and parenting, whose work has served as the foundation for this book. Your insights and wisdom have been a source of inspiration and a constant source of learning.

Lastly, I would like to thank my readers, who have taken the time to pick up this book and invest in their own growth as parents. Your commitment to nurturing the next generation and your desire to become better parents is what makes this journey all the more meaningful.

I am truly grateful for your support and I hope this book will provide you with the knowledge and tools you need to become the best parent you can be.

ACKNOWLEDGEMENTS

Parenting is a complex and challenging task that requires love, patience, and understanding. It is a journey that requires a commitment to nurturing and guiding the next generation. This book, "Nurturing the Next Generation: A Guide to Child Development and Parenting" is a comprehensive guide for parents and aspiring parents who want to understand and support their child's growth and development.

This book provides an in-depth look at the various aspects of child development, including physical, emotional, social, and cognitive growth. It covers important topics such as nutrition, sleep, emotional regulation, critical thinking, communication skills, and much more. The book also provides practical advice and strategies for building strong and positive relationships with your child, fostering independence and resilience, and navigating common parenting challenges.

The target audience for this book is anyone who is interested in enhancing their parenting skills and gaining a deeper understanding of child development. Whether you are a new parent, an experienced parent, or a grandparent, this book will provide valuable insights and guidance to help you become the best possible parent you can be.

It is my hope that this book will be a valuable resource for parents, providing them with the knowledge and tools they need to help their children reach their full potential. By understanding child development and applying best practices in parenting, we can work together to create a better future for our children and our world.

૎

Prologue

As a parent, one of the most important and fulfilling roles you will ever play is shaping and guiding the development of your child. From the moment they are born, you are given the opportunity to influence who they will become and what kind of life they will lead. It is a privilege, but it is also a great responsibility. There are so many different factors that can impact your child's growth and development, and it can be overwhelming to know where to start.

This book was written with the goal of providing parents with a comprehensive guide to child development and parenting. Our hope is that it will give you the knowledge, skills, and confidence you need to nurture and support your child as they grow and mature.

In these pages, you will find information about your child's physical, cognitive, emotional, and social development, as well as tips and strategies for raising a healthy and active child. We delve into child psychology, emotional development, and cognitive development, and provide guidance on building strong parent-child relationships, supporting your child's interests, and dealing with common parenting challenges.

Whether you are a seasoned parent, or just starting out on your journey, we hope that this book will be a valuable resource for you. Our aim is to help you raise confident, resilient, and responsible children who are prepared to thrive in the world.

We dedicate this book to all parents, and to the next generation of children who will benefit from their love and guidance. May it serve as a roadmap to help you navigate the many challenges of parenting and to find joy in the journey.

I
Introduction

Parenting is one of the most important and rewarding roles in life. It can also be one of the most challenging, especially as children grow and develop into their own individuals with unique personalities and needs.

As a parent, you have the opportunity to shape your child's life and lay the foundation for their future success. By providing love, support, and guidance, you can help your child reach their full potential and become a confident and capable adult.

This book aims to provide you with a comprehensive guide to child development and parenting. Through a combination of expert advice, practical tips, and personal experiences, you'll learn how to support your child's physical, emotional, and cognitive growth and build a strong, supportive relationship with them.

The purpose of this book is to provide an in-depth understanding of the various aspects of child development and to equip parents with the tools and strategies they need to raise happy, healthy, and well-rounded children. Our target audience is parents who are looking for practical guidance on how to support their children's growth and development.

You'll also discover how to navigate common parenting challenges and create a healthy and happy family environment for your child. Whether you're a new parent or an experienced one, this book offers insights and inspiration to help you become the best parent you can be.

This book is containing many real life examples of my daughter **"Sadhvi"** and as a parent my experiences, who has been raised with love and support and is now thriving at Isha Foundation, where she has learned important samskar. **Sadhvi** has been able to develop the skills and confidence to make her own decisions and lead a fulfilling life. My experiences as a parent, combined with expert knowledge and research, make this book a valuable resource for parents looking to support their children's growth and development.

A. Overview of the importance of parenting

Parenting is one of the most challenging and rewarding experiences a person can undertake. It requires a combination of love, patience, and a deep understanding of child development to help shape the next generation. From the moment a child is born, parents have a unique opportunity to influence their growth and development, helping them to become confident, responsible, and happy individuals.

As an example of the importance of parenting, we can look to the epic Hindu text, the Mahabharata. In the story, the Pandavas, five brothers, are raised with strong values, discipline, and love by their mother, Kunti. This upbringing helps them to become brave warriors and successful leaders, eventually triumphing in a great battle. The story demonstrates how the guidance and support provided by a parent can have a profound impact on a child's life.

A parent's role in a child's life is not just to provide love, care, and support, but also to guide them towards becoming independent and responsible individuals. In the epic Indian mythology of the Mahabharata, the Pandavas and Kauravas are examples of the influence of parenting on a child's upbringing. The Pandavas, who were raised with love, compassion, and strong moral values, went on to become just and noble rulers, while the Kauravas, who were raised with animosity and greed, were responsible for the great Kurukshetra war. This book, "Nurturing the Next Generation: A Guide to Child Development and Parenting" aims to help parents understand their role in their child's development and to provide practical tips on how to become better parents.

B. Purpose of the book

"Nurturing the Next Generation: A Guide to Child Development and Parenting," is to provide parents with a comprehensive understanding of child development and the skills and knowledge needed to become effective and supportive parents. By exploring the different stages of a child's physical, cognitive, emotional, and social development, this book aims to equip parents with the tools necessary to raise happy, healthy, and well-rounded children. Whether you are a first-time parent, an experienced parent looking for new insights, or a professional working with families, this book provides practical and research-based information to help you on your parenting journey.

જી

C. Target audience

This book is targeted towards parents, grandparents, guardians, and anyone who has a keen interest in nurturing and supporting the growth and development of children. Whether you're a first-time parent, have experience raising children, or have a passion for child development, this book offers insights and practical advice for all stages of a child's life. Whether you're looking to deepen your understanding of your child's physical, cognitive, emotional, and social development, or you want to learn more about building strong parent-child relationships and raising confident and responsible children, this guide has something for everyone

ॐ

II

Understanding Your Child's Development

In the second chapter of our book, we delve into the topic of Understanding Your Child's Development. The first aspect of this chapter is Physical Development. Physical development refers to the changes in the body structure and physical abilities of a child as they grow and mature. It encompasses a wide range of changes, from increased height and weight to improved coordination and dexterity. During the early years of a child's life, the most significant physical changes occur, including the development of motor skills and the growth of the brain and central nervous system. As children grow, they continue to refine their physical abilities and develop the strength, endurance, and coordination needed to participate in a wide range of activities.

A. Physical development

Physical development refers to the growth and maturation of a child's body, including changes in size, strength, coordination, and motor skills. Physical development begins at birth and continues throughout childhood and into adolescence. It is a critical aspect of overall child development and lays the foundation for future growth and success in other areas.

For example, in the Mahabharata, Prince Arjuna was renowned for his physical prowess and agility, as well as his mastery of weapons and combat techniques. He was able to use these skills to defend his kingdom and ultimately achieve victory in the great battle of Kurukshetra. By encouraging physical development, parents can help their children build the strength, coordination, and confidence they need to succeed in their own endeavors.

It is crucial for parents to understand their child's physical development and to provide opportunities for them to explore, play, and engage in physical activity. This helps to lay the foundation for a lifetime of good health and physical fitness. In the Mahabharata, we see examples of physical development being emphasized, such as when the Pandavas were trained in the art of warfare and physical fitness by their teacher, Dronacharya.

B. Cognitive development

Cognitive development refers to the growth and maturation of a person's mental processes and abilities, such as perception, attention, memory, language, problem solving, and reasoning. This is a field of study within psychology and developmental psychology, and the theory of cognitive development was popularized by Swiss psychologist Jean Piaget. The study of cognitive development is concerned with understanding how people acquire, process, store, and use information as they grow and age.

Additionally, cognitive development is considered a lifelong process that occurs in stages and is influenced by both biological and environmental factors. For example, genetics play a role in determining certain cognitive abilities, while a child's experiences and interactions with the world around them can shape their cognitive development. Understanding cognitive development is important as it can have implications for educational practices, as well as inform our understanding of the different ways that individuals process information and learn.

ಞ

C. Emotional and social development

Emotional and social development refers to the growth and change in a person's ability to recognize and regulate their own emotions, as well as understand and respond to the emotions of others. It involves the development of social skills, such as communication, empathy, cooperation, and attachment to others. This type of development occurs in parallel with cognitive development and is considered to be just as important for a child's overall well-being and success in life.

Emotional and social development is influenced by a variety of factors, including genetics, early life experiences, parenting practices, and social and cultural context. For example, children who grow up in stable, supportive environments with responsive caregivers are more likely to develop healthy emotional and social skills, while those who experience neglect or abuse may have difficulties in this area.

Just like cognitive development, emotional and social development is a lifelong process that continues to evolve and change throughout a person's life. Understanding and supporting this type of development is crucial for building healthy relationships and fostering personal growth and well-being.

⮺

D. How to support your child's development

Supporting your child's development is an important aspect of parenting, and there are many ways that you can help promote healthy growth and development in your child. Some tips for supporting your child's development include:

1. Provide a supportive and nurturing environment: This includes providing your child with stability, security, and affection, as well as opportunities for exploration and play.
2. Encourage exploration and play: Play is an essential part of children's development and helps them to build new skills and explore the world around them.
3. Foster a love of learning: Encourage your child's natural curiosity and help to create opportunities for learning and discovery.
4. Promote positive relationships: Encourage your child to form positive relationships with others, and model positive behaviors yourself.
5. Encourage healthy habits: Help your child develop healthy habits, such as regular exercise and good nutrition, that will support their overall health and well-being.
6. Support emotional regulation: Help your child learn to recognize and regulate their emotions, and provide opportunities for them to practice these skills.
7. Promote language development: Encourage your child's language development by speaking to them often, reading to them regularly, and providing opportunities for them to practice their communication skills.

It is important to remember that every child is unique and develops at their own pace. By providing a supportive and nurturing environment, you can help your child reach their full potential and thrive.

Providing a supportive and nurturing environment, as well as fulfilling your child's needs and desires in a responsible and age-appropriate way, can have a positive impact on their overall development. By taking this approach, you are helping your child to develop a sense of self-esteem, independence, and self-worth, which are important building blocks for their future success and well-being.

Additionally, educating your child and encouraging their natural curiosity is also an important aspect of supporting their development. By providing opportunities for learning and discovery, you are helping your child to develop critical thinking skills, problem-solving abilities, and a love of learning that will serve them well throughout their life.

Your approach to parenting, with a focus on support, education, and fulfillment of appropriate desires and needs, is a great way to help your child reach their full potential and thrive.

III

Raising a Healthy and Active Child

A.

Nutrition and meal planning

The foundation of good health begins with a balanced and nutritious diet. As a parent, it's important to provide your child with a variety of healthy foods that will fuel their growth and development. This includes foods from all food groups such as fruits and vegetables, whole grains, dairy, and lean protein sources. It's also important to establish mealtime routines and provide a positive eating environment.

As a parent, you want the best for your child and that includes providing them with a healthy and balanced diet. Good nutrition is essential for a child's growth and development, and what they eat can have a direct impact on their overall health and wellbeing. When raising your daughter Sadhvi, you were particularly conscious about the food you fed her. You were aware that the food regulates thoughts and directly affects a child's cognitive abilities and behavior. To ensure Sadhvi received the best nutrition possible, you made sure to provide her with nutritious and well-balanced meals that included a variety of fruits, vegetables, whole grains, lean proteins, and healthy fats. In addition, you made sure to limit sugary drinks and snacks and encouraged Sadhvi to drink plenty of water throughout the day. Overall, your focus on nutrition played a crucial role in helping Sadhvi grow and develop into a healthy and active child.

B. Physical activity and exercise

Physical activity and exercise are important components of a healthy lifestyle for children. Encouraging your child to engage in regular physical activity can help them maintain a healthy weight, build strong bones and muscles, improve cardiovascular health, and boost self-esteem. Some suggestions for promoting physical activity in your child include:

1. Lead by example: Children often mimic their parents' behavior, so make sure to engage in physical activity yourself and show your child how much fun it can be.
2. Make it fun: Encourage your child to participate in physical activities that they enjoy, such as playing sports, dancing, or going for walks.
3. Limit sedentary time: Limit the amount of time your child spends sitting or watching TV, and encourage them to take breaks and move around throughout the day.
4. Encourage outdoor play: Fresh air and outdoor play are important for children's physical and mental well-being. Encourage your child to play outside and explore their environment.
5. Try different activities: Encourage your child to try different types of physical activities, such as swimming, martial arts, or yoga, to keep them interested and engaged.

Remember, the goal is to help your child establish a lifetime habit of physical activity and exercise. With your support and encouragement, your child can learn to enjoy and value physical activity as a part of their daily routine.

∞

C. Sleep and Rest

1. Adequate sleep and rest are crucial components of a child's overall health and wellbeing.
2. During sleep, a child's body can repair and rejuvenate, while their brain processes and consolidates information learned during the day.
3. As a parent, it is important to establish a consistent sleep routine and ensure that your child is getting the recommended amount of sleep for their age.
4. You can establish a sleep routine by setting a consistent bedtime and waking time, creating a relaxing bedtime routine, and limiting exposure to screens and stimulating activities before bed.
5. You can also create a sleep-conducive environment by keeping the bedroom quiet, cool, and dark, and ensuring that the bed is comfortable.
6. It is also important to encourage your child to engage in physical activity and get plenty of exercise during the day, as this can help improve their sleep quality at night.
7. However, it is also important to balance physical activity with rest, and allow your child to take breaks and relax throughout the day.
8. By prioritizing sleep and rest, you can help ensure that your child has the energy and focus they need to reach their full potential.

മ

D. Dealing with common health issues

As a parent, it's important to be prepared to deal with common health issues that may arise in your child. Some steps you can take to keep your child healthy include:

- Regular check-ups: Regular check-ups with your child's doctor can help catch and prevent potential health problems.
- Proper nutrition: Encourage your child to eat a well-balanced diet that includes a variety of fruits, vegetables, whole grains, and lean proteins.
- Good hygiene: Teach your child good hygiene practices, such as regular hand washing, to prevent the spread of germs.
- Adequate sleep: Ensure your child gets enough sleep each night to promote overall health and well-being.
- Regular exercise: Regular exercise can help keep your child healthy and reduce the risk of many health problems.

If your child does become ill, it's important to seek prompt medical attention. Work with your child's doctor to determine the best course of treatment and to manage any ongoing health conditions. Remember, the goal is to keep your child healthy and active, so that they can grow and thrive.

જી

IV

Understanding Child Psychology

A. Overview of child psychology and its importance

Child psychology is a branch of psychology that focuses on the study of children's behavior, thoughts, and emotions, as well as the factors that influence their development. Understanding child psychology can play a crucial role in parenting, as it provides insight into a child's behavior, motivations, and responses to different situations.

Child psychology helps parents to understand the various stages of child development and the reasons behind a child's actions. It provides parents with the knowledge and tools to support their child's development and helps to create a positive and nurturing environment. With an understanding of child psychology, parents can also recognize and address any behavioral or emotional issues that may arise, leading to better outcomes for the child.

As a parent, it is important to understand the significance of child psychology and how it can impact the overall development of your child. By gaining insight into child psychology, you can better understand your child's behavior, thoughts, and emotions.

In your experience, you took a unique approach to parenting by considering my daughter Sadhvi's energy and needs. You were able to sense her desires and respond accordingly, using both your mind and heart. This type of intuitive parenting can help build a strong and healthy relationship between you and your child.

By incorporating an understanding of child psychology, you can create an environment that supports your child's physical, emotional, and mental growth. This will lay the foundation for a positive and fulfilling childhood, and set the stage for a successful future.

In conclusion, having an understanding of child psychology can be a valuable resource for parents, providing them with the knowledge to make informed decisions and support their child's healthy development.

As a parent, it is important to understand the significance of child psychology and how it can impact the overall development of your child. By gaining insight into child psychology, you can better understand your child's behavior, thoughts, and emotions.

In your experience, you took a unique approach to parenting by considering your daughter Sadhvi's energy and needs. You were able to sense her desires and respond accordingly, using both your mind and heart. This type of intuitive parenting can help build a strong and healthy relationship between you and your child.

By incorporating an understanding of child psychology, you can create an environment that supports your child's physical, emotional, and mental growth. This will lay the foundation for a positive and fulfilling childhood, and set the stage for a successful future.

જી

B. Key theories and concepts in child psychology

Child psychology is the scientific study of the cognitive, emotional, and social development of children. There are several key theories and concepts in child psychology that help to explain how children develop and grow. Some of these include:

1. Piaget's theory of cognitive development: This theory proposes that children develop through stages of cognitive development and that their thinking changes as they mature. This theory states that children go through four stages of cognitive development, starting with the sensorimotor stage (birth to 2 years), followed by the preoperational stage (2 to 7 years), concrete operational stage (7 to 11 years), and formal operational stage (11 years and above).

2. Erikson's theory of psychosocial development: This theory proposes that children develop through stages of psychosocial development and that their identity is shaped by their experiences and relationships. The theory proposes that children go through eight stages of psychosocial development, starting with trust vs. mistrust (birth to 1 year) and ending with integrity vs. despair (65 years and above). At each stage, children face a new challenge and must develop new skills to meet it.

3. Social learning theory: This theory suggests that children learn through observing and imitating the behavior of others. This theory suggests that children learn by observing and imitating the behavior of others, and that reinforcement (positive or negative) can influence the likelihood of continued behavior.

4. Attachment theory: This theory proposes that a child's early relationships with their caregivers have a lasting impact on their development and future relationships. This theory states that a child's early relationships with their caregivers have a lasting impact on their development and future relationships. A secure attachment helps to promote a child's overall well-being and future success.
5. Nature vs. Nurture: This concept refers to the debate about the relative importance of genetics (nature) and environment (nurture) in shaping a child's development. This concept refers to the idea that a child's development is influenced by both genetic factors (nature) and environmental factors (nurture).
6. Temperament: This refers to a child's inherent personality traits, such as their level of activity or impulsiveness. This refers to a child's innate personality traits, such as their level of activity or reactiveness, which are relatively stable over time and across situations.

These theories and concepts help to explain how children develop and grow, and provide a framework for understanding the complex processes of child development. However, it's important to note that every child is unique and may develop in their own way.

୫ଓ

C. How to apply child psychology principles to parenting

A. Understanding stages of development: Understanding the stages of cognitive, emotional, and social development can help you to set appropriate expectations for your child and respond to their needs in developmentally appropriate ways.

B. Encouraging exploration and experimentation: Children learn best through hands-on exploration and experimentation. Encourage your child to try new things and make mistakes, while providing a supportive and safe environment.

C. Nurturing attachment and relationships: Attachment and relationships are important for a child's overall development and well-being. Spend quality time with your child, and be responsive and supportive in their times of need.

D. Positive reinforcement: Children are more likely to repeat behaviors that are positively reinforced. Instead of solely using punishment to control behavior, focus on praising and encouraging positive behavior.

E. Consistency and structure: Children thrive on routine and consistency. By providing structure and routine, you can help your child to feel safe and secure.

F. Emotional intelligence: Helping your child to develop emotional intelligence can promote their overall well-being and success in life. Teach your child to recognize and manage their emotions, as well as to empathize with others.

By applying principles of child psychology to your parenting, you can help your child to reach their full potential and thrive. However, it's important to remember that every child is unique, and what works for one may not work for another.

જી

V
Emotional Development in Children

A. Understanding emotions in children

Emotions are an important aspect of a child's overall development and well-being. Understanding emotions in children involves recognizing the different emotions they experience, as well as their ability to understand, express, and regulate their emotions.

1. Recognizing emotions: Children's emotions can range from simple emotions like joy, sadness, and anger, to more complex emotions like guilt and embarrassment. As they grow and develop, they become more skilled at recognizing and expressing their emotions.
2. Understanding emotions: Children begin to develop an understanding of emotions in their early years. As they mature, they become better able to understand and label their emotions, as well as the emotions of others.

3. Expressing emotions: Children's ability to express their emotions can vary depending on their age, temperament, and experiences. Encouraging children to express their emotions in appropriate ways can help to promote their overall well-being and emotional regulation.

4. Regulating emotions: Children's ability to regulate their emotions improves as they grow and develop. However, some children may struggle with regulating their emotions, and may need support from adults.

5. By understanding emotions in children, parents and caregivers can better respond to their needs and support their overall emotional development. This can include helping children to understand their emotions, encouraging them to express their emotions in appropriate ways, and teaching them strategies for regulating their emotions.

B. Developing emotional regulation and coping skills

To help children develop emotional regulation and coping skills, you can provide a supportive and safe environment, teach them how to identify and express their emotions, and model appropriate coping strategies. Encourage children to practice mindfulness and relaxation techniques, such as deep breathing or progressive muscle relaxation. It's also important to help children understand that it's normal to have difficult emotions, and to teach them strategies for managing those emotions in healthy ways. This can include problem-solving, seeking support from trusted adults, and engaging in physical activity. Additionally, it may be helpful to seek outside support from a therapist or counselor if your child is struggling with emotional regulation.

❧

B. Developing emotional regulation and coping Skills

In "Emotional Development in Children" section, specifically in the subsection "Developing emotional regulation and coping skills," one could consider taking examples from the Hindu epic "Ramayana." The story of "Ramayana" is rich in themes related to emotions and coping skills, such as love, compassion, courage, perseverance, and resilience. For instance, Lord Rama demonstrates remarkable emotional regulation when faced with multiple challenges during his exile, and his wife Sita exemplifies perseverance and resilience when she is abducted by the demon king Ravana. These examples can serve as useful teaching tools for parents looking to help their children develop strong emotional regulation and coping skills. By discussing the emotions experienced by the characters in the story, parents can help their children understand and process their own emotions, leading to improved emotional regulation and resilience.

As a parent, it's important to understand the role you play in helping your child develop their emotional regulation and coping skills. One way to do this is by incorporating lessons and examples from mythology, such as the Hindu epic Ramayana. In the story, characters face various challenges and obstacles, but are able to overcome them through perseverance, resilience, and the use of their own inner strength. By teaching your child about these values, you can help them develop the emotional regulation and coping skills they need to navigate life's challenges with confidence and grace.

Encouraging emotional intelligence

1. Emotional intelligence refers to a person's ability to recognize, understand, and manage their own emotions, as well as the emotions of others. In children, developing emotional intelligence can help lay the foundation for healthy relationships, academic success, and overall well-being. Here are some tips for encouraging emotional intelligence in children:

2. Model emotional intelligence: Children learn by observing and imitating the people around them. Lead by example by showing empathy, managing your own emotions, and expressing feelings in an appropriate way.

3. Encourage emotional expression: Give children the space to express their feelings and validate their emotions. Avoid brushing their emotions aside or labeling them as "good" or "bad".

4. Teach empathy: Empathy is a crucial component of emotional intelligence. Encourage children to put themselves in others' shoes and think about how others might be feeling.

5. Foster problem-solving skills: Help children develop problem-solving skills so they can learn to manage their emotions and resolve conflicts in a healthy way.

6. Provide opportunities for emotional regulation: Teach children techniques for regulating their emotions, such as deep breathing, counting to 10, or visualization.

Overall, emotional intelligence can be developed through nurturing relationships, positive reinforcement, and intentional teaching. By encouraging emotional intelligence in children, you can set them up for success in all areas of their lives.

D. Dealing with anxiety and depression in children

1. Dealing with anxiety and depression in children can be challenging, but early intervention can help children learn coping skills that can improve their mental health and overall well-being. Here are some real-time examples of how to deal with anxiety and depression in children:

2. Encourage open communication: Create an environment where children feel comfortable talking about their emotions and thoughts. Encourage them to express themselves and listen actively to what they have to say.

3. Normalize emotions: Explain to children that everyone experiences anxiety and depression at some point in their lives. Emphasize that these feelings are normal and can be managed.

4. Help them identify triggers: Work with children to identify what triggers their anxiety or depression. This can help them learn to recognize and manage these emotions when they arise.

5. Teach coping skills: Teach children healthy coping mechanisms, such as deep breathing, mindfulness, or physical activity, to help manage their emotions.

6. Connect them with resources: If your child is struggling with anxiety or depression, connect them with a mental health professional or support group.

7. Maintain routine and structure: Consistency and structure can help children feel secure and reduce anxiety. Encourage a consistent bedtime routine, meal schedule, and physical activity.

8. Foster a positive mindset: Encourage children to focus on their strengths and positive experiences, and help them develop a growth mindset by focusing on progress and effort rather than

perfection.

VI
Cognitive Development in Children

A. Understanding cognitive development

Cognitive development refers to the process of growth and change in children's ability to think, understand, and remember information. It encompasses a wide range of abilities, including perception, attention, memory, language, problem-solving, and decision-making. Cognitive development occurs in a predictable sequence and is influenced by both genetic and environmental factors.

The most widely recognized theory of cognitive development is that of Swiss psychologist Jean Piaget, who proposed that children progress through four stages of cognitive development: sensorimotor, preoperational, concrete operational, and formal operational. During each stage, children's thinking and understanding of the world become more complex and sophisticated.

It's important to understand cognitive development in children because it can inform educational practices and help parents and caregivers support children's growth and development. By providing appropriate and stimulating experiences, children can continue to develop their cognitive abilities, which can have a positive impact on their academic, social, and emotional development.

Here are some real-time examples of how cognitive development manifests in children:

1. Sensorimotor stage (birth to 2 years): During this stage, children use their senses and motor skills to understand the world around them. For example, a baby might explore their surroundings by putting objects in their mouth or grabbing onto things.

2. Preoperational stage (2 to 7 years): During this stage, children begin to understand symbols, such as words and numbers. For example, a child might recognize that a picture of a dog represents a dog, or understand that the number "3" stands for three objects.

3. Concrete operational stage (7 to 11 years): During this stage, children develop logical thinking and can solve concrete problems. For example, a child might be able to compare the height of two objects, or understand that adding three blocks to five blocks results in eight blocks.

4. Formal operational stage (11 years and up): During this stage, children develop abstract reasoning and can think logically about theoretical or hypothetical situations. For example, a teenager might be able to understand and analyze a complex argument or think about the ethical implications of a situation.

ॐ

B. Encouraging critical thinking and problem-solving skills

Encouraging critical thinking and problem-solving skills in children is important for their cognitive development and future success. Here are some ways to encourage these skills in children:

1. Encourage exploration and play: Play allows children to experiment, discover, and solve problems in a safe and supportive environment. Encourage open-ended play, such as building with blocks or playing with playdough, to foster creativity and problem-solving skills.
2. Ask open-ended questions: Ask questions that encourage children to think critically and consider multiple perspectives. Avoid yes/no questions and instead encourage children to explain their reasoning and thought process.
3. Provide opportunities for decision-making: Give children opportunities to make decisions, such as choosing what to wear or what to have for breakfast. This helps them practice problem-solving and critical thinking skills.
4. Foster a growth mindset: Encourage children to embrace challenges and see mistakes as opportunities for growth. This can help them develop resilience and a willingness to tackle difficult problems.
5. Encourage collaboration: Group activities and projects can help children learn to work together, communicate, and solve problems as a team. Encourage children to work together to find solutions and compromise when necessary.
6. Teach critical thinking strategies: Teach children strategies for critical thinking and problem-solving, such as breaking a problem down into smaller parts, generating multiple

solutions, and evaluating the potential outcomes of each solution.

1. Encourage different perspectives: Encourage children to consider different viewpoints and look at problems from multiple angles. This can help them develop empathy and understand that there is often more than one solution to a problem.
2. Foster creativity: Encourage children to use their imagination and come up with new and innovative ideas. This can help them develop their problem-solving skills and think outside the box.
3. Provide hands-on learning experiences: Hands-on activities, such as building projects or cooking, can help children develop their problem-solving skills by giving them the opportunity to apply what they have learned in real-world situations.
4. Encourage experimentation: Encourage children to test out their ideas and experiment with different solutions. This helps them develop their critical thinking skills and learn from their mistakes.

※

C. Supporting language and literacy development

When it comes to supporting language and literacy development in children, it's important to create a supportive environment from an early age. This can include reading to them regularly, engaging in conversation and asking questions to encourage language and critical thinking skills, and providing educational toys and activities that promote language and literacy development.

For example, when my daughter Sadhvi was young, I made a habit of reading to her every night before bed. This not only helped her develop a love for books and storytelling, but also helped her expand her vocabulary and improve her listening and comprehension skills. Additionally, I also made a point to ask her open-ended questions and encourage her to express herself, which helped her build confidence in her communication skills. Furthermore, I provided educational toys and games that encouraged her to learn letters and words, which laid a strong foundation for her future success in reading and writing.

☙

Helping children with learning challenges

Understanding and supporting children with learning challenges is an important aspect of parenting. Children with learning challenges face difficulties in acquiring, processing and retaining information, which can affect their academic performance and self-esteem. To help children with learning challenges, parents can follow some key steps. Firstly, it is important to understand the specific learning challenge that your child is facing, whether it be dyslexia, ADHD, or another condition. This can be done through an evaluation by a specialist or teacher. Once the challenge is identified, parents can work with their child's teacher and other professionals to develop an individualized plan that takes into account their child's strengths and weaknesses. This may include using assistive technologies, providing extra support in the classroom, or adapting learning materials to suit the child's needs. Additionally, parents can also provide a supportive and encouraging environment at home and reinforce the child's self-esteem by praising their efforts and accomplishments. By taking these steps, parents can help their child overcome their learning challenges and build the skills they need to succeed.

☙

VII
Building Strong Parent-Child Relationships

A. Communication skills

Good communication is key to building strong relationships with our children, and this includes our relationship with our daughter, Sadhvi. As a parent, it's important to actively listen to your child, acknowledge their feelings and perspectives, and respond in a way that is supportive and understanding. This can help to build trust, foster a positive relationship, and encourage open and honest communication between parent and child. In order to support your child's communication skills and build a strong relationship with them, it's important to be a good role model, using clear and respectful language, avoiding criticism, and encouraging active listening and empathy.

B. Setting limits and boundaries

As a parent, setting limits and boundaries is an important aspect of raising a well-rounded and disciplined child. In my experience raising my daughter Sadhvi, I found that it was essential to clearly communicate what was expected of her in terms of behavior and to consistently enforce consequences when those expectations were not met. This helped her understand the importance of responsibility and accountability and taught her to make better choices.

However, it was also important to balance this structure with empathy and understanding. I made sure to listen to Sadhvi's perspectives and to explain why certain rules and boundaries were in place, which helped her feel respected and valued. Through this approach, I was able to build a strong and positive relationship with my daughter based on trust, respect, and open communication.

❧

C. Encouraging independence

As a parent, encouraging independence in your child is crucial for their growth and development. One way to foster independence is to allow them to make their own decisions, within reason, and to learn from the consequences of their choices. This helps them to develop their problem-solving skills and to build confidence in their abilities.

My daughter Sadhvi was no exception to this. From a young age, I encouraged her to be independent and make her own decisions. For instance, I allowed her to choose what she wanted to wear, within the boundaries of appropriateness, and to help with household chores. This helped her to develop a sense of responsibility and to understand the importance of contributing to the family.

The Upanishads emphasize the importance of self-reliance and independence in one's life. They teach that each person has the power within themselves to achieve their goals and to live a fulfilling life. By encouraging independence in Sadhvi, I was helping her to develop this important aspect of her character and to prepare her for a successful future.

౭౩

D. Quality time with your child

One of the most important aspects of building a strong relationship with your child is spending quality time together. This can be done through simple activities such as playing games, reading books, taking walks, or simply sitting down to chat. By creating special moments with your child, you are not only building strong bonds, but also helping your child to feel valued, loved, and supported.

It's important to remember that quality time doesn't have to be expensive or time-consuming. The most important factor is that the time spent together is focused and intentional. This means putting away distractions, such as phones and computers, and fully engaging with your child.

For example, in the epic Indian ramyana, King Janaka was known for his strong relationships with his children. He would regularly spend time with them, teaching them valuable lessons and sharing his wisdom. This deep connection with his children allowed him to guide them to become wise, virtuous leaders in their own right.

By prioritizing quality time with your child, you can help build a strong foundation for a lasting and meaningful relationship.

೮೨

VIII

Supporting Your Child's Interests and Passions

A. Finding and encouraging your child's interests

Finding and encouraging your child's interests can play a significant role in their overall development and happiness. Here are a few tips to help you support your child's interests:

1. Observe: Pay attention to what your child is naturally drawn to, what they enjoy doing and what they are good at.
2. Provide opportunities: Offer a range of activities and experiences for your child to try and explore their interests.
3. Encourage: Show interest and support for your child's passions, no matter how unconventional they may be.
4. Be patient: Children's interests may change over time, so be patient and continue to support them as they grow and explore.
5. Foster independence: Encourage your child to take initiative and make decisions about their interests. This helps build self-esteem and confidence.

Remember, every child is unique, and what may be interesting for one child, may not be for another. The important thing is to provide a supportive environment that encourages exploration, learning, and growth.

B. Balancing structured activities and free play

Balancing structured activities and free play is an important aspect of supporting your child's interests and passions. Both types of activities have their own benefits and it's essential to find a balance that works best for your child.

Structured activities such as sports, music lessons, or clubs can provide children with structure, discipline, and opportunities to develop skills in specific areas.

On the other hand, free play is essential for a child's overall development. It allows them to use their imagination, explore their environment, and practice decision-making and problem-solving skills.

Here are a few tips to help balance structured activities and free play:

1. Limit structured activities: Avoid over-scheduling your child. Encourage them to have plenty of free time to play and explore.
2. Encourage free play: Provide opportunities for your child to engage in unstructured play, such as playing with friends, playing outside, or participating in imaginative play.
3. Prioritize quality over quantity: Focus on quality experiences, rather than the number of activities your child is involved in.
4. Respect their interests: Support your child's interests, even if they may not align with your own.
5. Listen to your child: Pay attention to your child's feelings and reactions to different activities. If they are feeling overwhelmed or uninterested, it may be time to adjust the balance between

structured activities and free play.

By balancing structured activities and free play, you can help your child develop their interests and passions in a way that is healthy and sustainable.

C. Supporting your child's creative pursuits

Supporting your child's creative pursuits is important for their overall development and well-being. Here are a few tips for encouraging and supporting your child's creative interests:

1. Provide resources: Make sure your child has the tools and materials they need to pursue their creative interests, whether that's art supplies, musical instruments, or writing materials.
2. Create an environment that fosters creativity: Encourage your child to express themselves freely and provide a safe and supportive environment for their creative pursuits.
3. Celebrate their successes: Recognize and celebrate your child's creative achievements, no matter how small they may seem. This builds self-esteem and confidence.
4. Respect their process: Let your child take the lead in their creative pursuits, even if it doesn't align with your own artistic vision or preferences.

As an example, Sachin Tendulkar's parents supported his passion for cricket from a young age. They recognized his talent and provided him with the resources and opportunities he needed to pursue his passion. As a result, he went on to become one of the greatest cricketers of all time.

Remember, every child is unique and has their own creative interests and talents. By supporting your child's creative pursuits, you can help them develop their passions and build a strong foundation for a fulfilling and successful life.

છ

D. Helping your child find their passion

Helping your child find their passion can be a challenging but rewarding process. Here are a few tips to get started:

1. Encourage exploration: Encourage your child to try new activities and explore different interests.
2. Provide opportunities: Offer a range of experiences and activities that will help your child discover what they are interested in and passionate about.
3. Foster creativity: Encourage your child to be creative and explore their imagination. This can help them develop their passions and find their niche.
4. Be supportive: Show interest in your child's pursuits, listen to their ideas and offer guidance and support when needed.

As an example, APJ Abdul Kalam was passionate about science and technology from a young age. His family encouraged his interests and provided him with the resources and opportunities he needed to pursue his passion. As a result, he went on to become a renowned scientist and the President of India.

Finding a passion can be a journey, and it's essential to be patient and supportive along the way. By providing opportunities and encouragement, you can help your child discover what they love and set them on a path towards a fulfilling and successful life.

☙

IX
Raising Responsible and Confident Children

A. Building self-esteem

Building self-esteem in children is an important aspect of raising responsible and confident children. Self-esteem is a child's belief in their own abilities and worth as a person. A child with high self-esteem is more likely to be resilient, confident, and better able to cope with challenges.

One example of a person who was raised with a focus on building self-esteem is Narendra Modi, the current Prime Minister of India. From a young age, Modi's parents emphasized the importance of hard work, discipline, and self-reliance. They encouraged him to take on responsibilities and pursue his interests, and they recognized and celebrated his achievements.

By providing a supportive and encouraging environment, Modi's parents helped him develop his self-esteem and confidence. This foundation served him well throughout his life, as he went on to become a successful political leader and advocate for the people of India.

Building self-esteem in children requires a combination of support, recognition, and encouragement. Parents can help their children develop self-esteem by providing opportunities for success, recognizing and celebrating their accomplishments, and helping them to see their own strengths and abilities. By taking an active role in building their child's self-esteem, parents can set them on a path towards a successful and fulfilling life.

B. Teaching responsibility

Teaching responsibility is an important part of raising responsible and confident children. By teaching children to be responsible, parents can help them develop a sense of accountability and prepare them for the challenges of adulthood.

One example of a child who has been taught responsibility is my daughter, Sadhvi. To help her develop responsibility, you may have given her tasks and chores to do around the house, encouraged her to take on responsibilities at school or in her community, and held her accountable for her actions.

By giving Sadhvi responsibilities and helping her understand the consequences of her actions, you are teaching her important life skills and helping her to become a responsible and confident young person. As she continues to grow and mature, these skills will serve her well and help her succeed in all areas of her life.

Teaching responsibility is an ongoing process that requires patience, consistency, and a commitment to helping children develop the skills they need to be successful. By taking an active role in teaching responsibility, parents can help their children develop the confidence and accountability they need to become responsible and successful adults.

৪০

C. Encouraging positive behavior

Encouraging positive behavior in children is an important aspect of raising responsible and confident children. Positive behavior can include being respectful, responsible, and kind to others. By encouraging these behaviors, parents can help their children develop strong social skills and a positive attitude towards themselves and others.

One example of a person who encourages positive behavior is Sadhguru, the founder of Isha Foundation. Sadhguru has a strong commitment to helping people lead more fulfilling lives and has worked to create programs and initiatives that encourage positive behavior and personal growth.

Through his teachings and programs, Sadhguru emphasizes the importance of mindfulness, compassion, and self-awareness. He encourages people to be present in the moment, to treat others with kindness and respect, and to lead lives of purpose and meaning.

Encouraging positive behavior is an essential part of raising responsible and confident children. By teaching children to be mindful, compassionate, and respectful, parents can help them develop strong social skills and a positive attitude towards themselves and others. This foundation will serve them well throughout their lives and help them succeed in all areas of their lives.

☙

D. Dealing with misbehavior

Dealing with misbehavior is a challenging aspect of raising responsible and confident children. It is important for parents to address misbehavior in a constructive and supportive manner, so that children can learn from their mistakes and develop positive behavior patterns.

One example of a person who experienced the consequences of misbehavior as a child is Elon Musk, the CEO of Tesla and SpaceX. Musk has spoken publicly about his experiences growing up and how his parents dealt with his misbehavior.

According to Musk, his parents were strict and held him accountable for his actions. They encouraged him to take responsibility for his mistakes and to work to correct his behavior. They also provided him with structure and support, helping him to develop the discipline and determination that would serve him well throughout his life.

Dealing with misbehavior requires a balance of firmness and support. Parents can help their children learn from their mistakes by holding them accountable for their actions, providing structure and support, and helping them to develop positive behavior patterns. By doing so, they can help their children become responsible and confident adults.

☙

X
Navigating Common Parenting Challenges

A. Discipline strategies

Discipline is an important aspect of parenting and an effective discipline strategy can help children develop self-control and make positive choices. Effective discipline strategies can vary based on the child's age, personality, and the specific behavior that needs to be addressed.

One example of a person who experienced effective discipline as a child is Narendra Modi, the Prime Minister of India. Growing up, Modi's parents were strict and held him accountable for his actions. They encouraged him to take responsibility for his mistakes and to work to correct his behavior.

Modi has spoken publicly about the impact his parents' discipline had on his life, saying that their strict but supportive approach helped him develop discipline and determination. He has credited this discipline with helping him to achieve his goals and become a successful leader.

Effective discipline strategies can help children develop self-control and make positive choices. It is important for parents to find a balance between firmness and support and to adapt their discipline strategies to meet the needs of their child. By doing so, they can help their children become responsible and confident adults.

In addition to being strict and supportive, effective discipline strategies should also be consistent and fair. Children need to understand the rules and the consequences for breaking them, and they should feel that the consequences are appropriate for their misbehavior.

Positive reinforcement is also an effective discipline strategy, where parents reward good behavior and provide praise and encouragement. This can help children feel valued and motivated to continue making positive choices.

It is also important for parents to model positive behavior and to be consistent in their own behavior. Children learn by observing the people around them and by imitating the behavior they see. By showing respect, kindness, and responsibility, parents can help their children develop these same values and behavior patterns.

In some cases, misbehavior may be a symptom of underlying problems such as stress, anxiety, or frustration. In these cases, it is important for parents to understand the root cause of the misbehavior and to work with their child to address it.

B. Sibling rivalry

Sibling rivalry is a common challenge that many families face, as siblings often compete for attention, resources, and affection. This can lead to conflicts and negative behavior, and can be difficult for parents to navigate.

One example of sibling rivalry is the relationship between Duryodhana and his siblings in Hindu mythology. In the Mahabharata, Duryodhana was jealous of his elder siblings and felt that he was not being treated fairly. This led to conflicts and resentment between Duryodhana and his siblings, which eventually escalated into a devastating war.

Sibling rivalry can be a challenging aspect of parenting, but it is important for parents to address it in a constructive and positive way. This may involve setting clear rules, providing individual attention and resources, and teaching siblings to communicate effectively and resolve conflicts in a peaceful manner. By doing so, parents can help their children develop positive relationships with their siblings and avoid negative behavior.

ॐ

D. Handling stress and burnout

Handling stress and burnout is a major challenge for many parents, especially working parents who often juggle the demands of work, family, and personal responsibilities. In today's fast-paced world, it is more important than ever for parents to find ways to manage their stress and avoid burnout.

Working parents face unique challenges when it comes to stress and burnout. They often have limited time and resources to devote to their families, and they must balance the demands of work with the needs of their children. To manage stress and avoid burnout, it is important for working parents to prioritize self-care, set realistic expectations, and find support from others.

One approach to managing stress and avoiding burnout is to set aside time each day for activities that promote physical, emotional, and mental well-being. This may include exercise, mindfulness practices, or engaging in hobbies and interests. It is also important for working parents to prioritize their relationships and seek support from friends, family, or community resources.

Handling stress and avoiding burnout is a major challenge for working parents. By prioritizing self-care, setting realistic expectations, and seeking support from others, working parents can manage their stress and avoid burnout, and provide the best possible care for their children.

ೞ

XI

Navigating the Teen Years

A. Understanding teenage development

Adolescence can be a challenging time for both parents and children. During this stage, children face physical, emotional, and cognitive changes that can affect their behaviour and attitudes. Sania Mirza, the famous tennis player, serves as a great example of how adolescence can shape an individual's future success. Sania's dedication, hard work, and perseverance during her teenage years helped her become a successful professional athlete. As parents, it is important to understand the complexities of teenage development and support our children through this transitional period. By providing guidance, encouragement, and love, we can help our children navigate this crucial stage and lay the foundation for their future success.

During the teenage years, children experience significant physical, emotional, and psychological changes. They are developing a sense of self and seeking independence. One example of a successful individual who navigated these challenges is tennis player Sania Mirza. She started playing tennis at a young age and rose to fame as a successful athlete while navigating the challenges of teenage development. Her dedication and hard work, along with the support of her family, allowed her to become one of India's most successful tennis players. By following her story and others like hers, parents can gain insight into how to support their teens as they navigate the complex and often confusing process of growing up.

B. Building trust and open communication

Building trust and open communication with your teen is crucial for a healthy parent-child relationship. This can help teens feel supported and understood, and can make it easier for parents to address any challenges or problems that may arise.

For example, as my daughter Sadhvi navigates the teen years, as her parent I can focus on building trust and open communication with her. This might involve regularly checking in with Sadhvi to see how she is doing and to encourage her to share her thoughts and feelings. Additionally, parents can also model open and honest communication themselves, and avoid being critical or dismissive of Sadhvi's perspective.

Another important aspect of building trust and open communication is setting boundaries and rules that are fair and consistent. This can help teens understand what is expected of them, and can provide a sense of stability and security. At the same time, parents should also be flexible and willing to listen to their teen's perspective, and to make adjustments as needed.

Building trust and open communication with your teen is essential for a healthy parent-child relationship. By focusing on active listening, honesty, and consistency, parents can help their teens feel supported and understood, and build a strong foundation for their relationship.

୫୬

C. Dealing with peer pressure and bullying

Dealing with peer pressure and bullying is a common challenge for many teens, including those in the public eye. For example, many film stars have faced peer pressure and bullying during their teenage years.

To help teens navigate these challenges, it is important for parents to provide support and guidance. This might involve teaching teens how to recognize and resist peer pressure, and helping them build self-esteem and confidence. Additionally, parents can also help their teens identify safe and positive peer groups, and encourage them to spend time with friends who support and respect them.

It is also important for parents to address bullying when it occurs. This might involve teaching teens how to respond to bullying in a assertive and confident manner, and encouraging them to report bullying to a trusted adult. Additionally, parents can also work with schools and other organizations to address bullying and promote a positive and inclusive environment.

In conclusion, dealing with peer pressure and bullying is a major challenge for many teens, including film stars. By providing support, guidance, and a positive environment, parents can help their teens navigate these challenges and build the skills and confidence they need to succeed.

D. Preparing for independence and adulthood

The teen years are an important time for preparing young people for independence and adulthood. Here are some steps to help prepare your teen:

1. Encourage them to take on responsibilities and make decisions
2. Teach them life skills such as budgeting, cooking, and time management
3. Help them develop a strong work ethic and encourage them to pursue their interests and passions
4. Foster their independence by giving them more freedom to make decisions and solve problems on their own
5. Discuss with them the challenges and opportunities of adulthood, such as paying bills, finding a job, and maintaining relationships
6. Encourage them to start thinking about their future goals, both short-term and long-term
7. Teach them about healthy relationships and the importance of communication, trust, and respect
8. Discuss with them the dangers of drugs and alcohol and the importance of making healthy choices.

ॐ

XII
Raising Confident and Resilient Children

A. Building resilience

Resilience is the ability to cope with challenges, difficulties, and setbacks in life. Here are some ways to help build resilience in children:

1. Encourage them to take healthy risks and face challenges
2. Teach them problem-solving skills
3. Foster a growth mindset and positive self-talk
4. Promote their independence and self-reliance
5. Support their relationships with friends and family
6. Help them find meaning and purpose in their lives
7. Teach them to manage emotions and stress in healthy ways
8. Encourage them to be grateful and to practice kindness and empathy. Teach them to bounce back from failure and to view it as an opportunity for growth
9. Encourage them to have a positive outlook and to look for solutions instead of dwelling on problems
10. Help them develop strong coping skills and self-care habits

11. Support their autonomy and encourage them to make decisions and take responsibility for their actions

12. Encourage them to have a strong support network of family, friends, and mentors

13. Teach them to be flexible and adaptable to change

14. Help them understand and manage their emotions by teaching them healthy ways to express them.

15. The teen years are an important time for preparing young people for independence and adulthood. Here are some steps to help prepare your teen:

B. Coping with disappointment and failure

Helping children cope with disappointment and failure is an important aspect of raising confident and resilient children. Here are some ways to do so:

1. Teach them that failure is a natural part of the learning process and a stepping stone to success.
2. Encourage them to persevere in the face of setbacks and to keep trying until they achieve their goals.
3. Teach them problem-solving skills and to look for solutions instead of dwelling on problems.
4. Help them develop a growth mindset and to view challenges as opportunities for growth.
5. Encourage them to take healthy risks and to not be afraid of failure.
6. Teach them to manage their emotions and to not let disappointment and failure define them.
7. Encourage them to have a positive outlook and to focus on their strengths and abilities.
8. Provide support and encouragement, and help them see the bigger picture.

ଔ

C. Encouraging a growth mindset

Encouraging a growth mindset in children can help them become more confident and resilient. A growth mindset is the belief that abilities and intelligence can be developed through hard work, effort, and learning. Here are some ways to encourage a growth mindset in children:

- Celebrate their effort and hard work, not just their achievements.
- Encourage them to embrace challenges and view them as opportunities for growth.
- Teach them that intelligence and abilities can be developed through practice and learning.
- Help them develop a positive self-talk and to focus on their strengths.
- Provide constructive feedback that emphasizes the process of learning and growth.
- Encourage them to persevere in the face of setbacks and to keep trying until they achieve their goals.
- Celebrate their progress, no matter how small, and help them see their progress over time.
- Teach them to be flexible and adaptable to change, and to view failure as an opportunity for growth.

∞

D. Supporting mental health and wellness

Supporting mental health and wellness in children involves fostering open communication, teaching healthy coping skills, promoting physical activity and healthy eating, and recognizing and addressing any mental health concerns early on.

Regarding Elon Musk's mother, it is reported that she taught him to read at a young age, which helped him develop a love for learning and a strong foundation for future success. She also encouraged his creativity and provided a supportive environment that allowed him to pursue his interests and passions. By providing a supportive and nurturing environment, she played a key role in shaping Elon Musk's confidence and resilience, which have served him well in his personal and professional life.

In addition to the above, here are some more ways to support mental health and wellness:

- Encourage physical activity and healthy eating habits.
- Teach them to manage stress and handle emotions in a healthy way.
- Foster a positive self-image and self-esteem.
- Provide a stable and supportive home environment.
- Encourage them to seek help when needed and to not be afraid to talk about their feelings and emotions.
- Teach them to recognize and manage any mental health concerns, such as anxiety or depression.
- Encourage them to pursue their interests and passions and to have a positive outlook on life.

- Provide them with a strong support network of family, friends, and mentors.

ଚଛ

XIII

13. Conclusion Recap of key takeaways

In the conclusion of "Nurturing the Next Generation: A Guide to Child Development and Parenting," the key takeaways can be summarized as follows:

A. Recap of Key Takeaways:

1. Parenting is a critical aspect of child development and has a profound impact on a child's physical, cognitive, emotional, and social well-being.
2. Understanding your child's development involves paying attention to their physical, cognitive, emotional, and social development and providing the support and resources they need to thrive.
3. Raising a healthy and active child requires a focus on nutrition, physical activity, sleep, and addressing common health issues.
4. Child psychology is a crucial tool for parents to understand their child's behavior and emotions, and to create a supportive and nurturing environment.
5. Emotional development in children requires an understanding of emotions and the development of emotional regulation and

coping skills, as well as encouraging emotional intelligence.

6. Cognitive development in children involves fostering critical thinking and problem-solving skills, supporting language and literacy, and addressing learning challenges.

7. Building strong parent-child relationships involves effective communication, setting limits and boundaries, fostering independence, and spending quality time with your child.

8. Supporting your child's interests and passions involves finding and encouraging their interests, balancing structured activities and free play, and fostering their creative pursuits.

9. Raising responsible and confident children requires building self-esteem, teaching responsibility, encouraging positive behavior, and addressing misbehavior.

10. Navigating common parenting challenges involves using effective discipline strategies, navigating potty training, sibling rivalry, and stress and burnout.

11. Navigating the teen years involves understanding teenage development, building trust and open communication, addressing peer pressure and bullying, and preparing for independence and adulthood.

12. Raising confident and resilient children involves building resilience, coping with disappointment and failure, encouraging a growth mindset, and supporting mental health and wellness.

B. Final thoughts on the importance of parenting

Parenting is a journey that requires patience, persistence, and a commitment to continuous learning and growth. By following the principles and strategies outlined in this book, parents can create a supportive and nurturing environment that will help their children thrive.

Parenting is one of the most important and rewarding roles that one can undertake in life. It requires patience, commitment, and an understanding of child development and psychology. The purpose of this book has been to provide parents with a comprehensive guide to child development and parenting, covering everything from physical and cognitive development to building strong parent-child relationships and supporting mental health and wellness. The key takeaways from this book include the importance of providing a healthy and active lifestyle, encouraging emotional regulation and intelligence, promoting independence and responsibility, and fostering resilience and a growth mindset in children. Additionally, it is important to communicate effectively, build trust, and navigate common parenting challenges such as discipline, peer pressure, and the teenage years. Ultimately, the goal of parenting is to help children become confident, responsible, and successful adults. By continuing to learn and grow as a parent, one can be better equipped to support the next generation and help them reach their full potential.

૪૭

C. Encouragement and resources for continued learning and growth.

The goal of this book is to provide parents with the knowledge and skills they need to be effective and confident parents. For continued learning and growth, parents are encouraged to seek out additional resources and support. These may include parenting classes, support groups, books, websites, and other resources that can help them on their journey.

Parenting is a lifelong journey that requires ongoing learning and growth. As children grow and change, it is essential for parents to stay informed and seek out new resources and support. The conclusion of this book is just the beginning of the journey, and there are many opportunities for continued learning and growth. There are numerous resources available to parents, including books, online forums, workshops, and support groups. Additionally, speaking with other parents and professionals can provide valuable insights and perspectives on child development and parenting. To further encourage continued learning and growth, it is important to remain open to new ideas and approaches, and to be willing to adjust your parenting style as your child grows and changes. By embracing this lifelong journey and taking advantage of the many resources available, parents can become confident and effective in their role as a nurturer and guide for the next generation.

છ

Top 25 Tips From My Side To Become The Great Parent!

Finally Nurturing the Next Generation the top 25 tips from my side to become the great parent!

1. Be a good role model for your children
2. Show love and affection towards your children
3. Listen to your children and try to understand their perspective
4. Be consistent with rules and discipline
5. Provide a safe and stable environment for your children
6. Encourage independence and encourage your children to take risks
7. Teach your children important life skills
8. Foster a positive self-esteem in your children
9. Provide opportunities for your children to learn and explore their interests
10. Be patient and understanding with your children
11. Encourage open communication with your children
12. Show interest in your children's activities and hobbies
13. Lead by example and teach good values and morals
14. Encourage physical activity and outdoor play
15. Set limits and boundaries for your children, while allowing them to make mistakes and learn from them
16. Practice positive reinforcement and praise your children for their efforts and achievements
17. Be involved in your children's education and support their academic success
18. Encourage healthy relationships with family and friends
19. Teach your children to be respectful towards others
20. Foster a love for nature and the environment
21. Promote creativity and encourage artistic expression
22. Teach your children how to handle emotions and stress in a healthy manner

23. Help your children develop critical thinking and problem-solving skills
24. Foster a sense of community and volunteerism in your children
25. Celebrate your children's successes, big and small, and support them through their challenges.

TO CONNET WITH US

To attend all out parenting programs you can connect with us
Mobile 6364795551 / 9538735551